Looking after my pet

Hamster

DAVID ALDERTON

LORENZ BOOKS

Introduction

Having a pet hamster is great fun. But before you get a hamster, ask yourself – do you have time to look after a pet? Hamsters must be fed and given clean water every day. You will also need to clean out your hamster's home twice a week and wash it every two weeks. Then, you must remember to buy all the things that your hamster needs, such as its food and bedding. You will also have to spend time making friends with your hamster and playing with it for a few minutes each evening.

You'll need to think about where you can put your hamster's home.

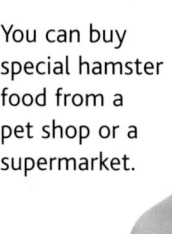

You can buy special hamster food from a pet shop or a supermarket.

A caring owner

It is not difficult to care for a hamster, and you will be able to do this on your own most of the time, but sometimes you will need help from an adult. Hamsters are much easier to look after than some pets, because they live indoors and do not need to be taken out for walks. It takes only a few minutes each day to give your hamster food and water, and even cleaning out the cage takes less than 10 minutes.

A family pet

Hamsters can become special pets for everyone in the family. If you let other people help you look after your hamster, this will mean less work for you! Sharing your pet like this is actually a good idea, because other members of your family will know how to take care of your pet when you are away, without you having to tell them. Your hamster will also be used to them, and so it will not miss you as much.

Looking after a hamster can be fun for all the family.

Taming your hamster will be fun. Be careful not to get bitten, though!

A happy home

Even if you live in an apartment, where you can't have a dog, a hamster will be completely happy. Hamsters are quiet and won't disturb your neighbors. They sleep through the day and wake up in the late afternoon, when you get home from school. This means that your hamster will not be lonely when you leave it on its own during the day.

Don't cramp your pet in a small home. A cage this size may not be big enough for your hamster to run around in.

What is a hamster?

Hamsters are small, furry animals with short tails. There are 16 different types of wild hamster in the world. They live in the Middle East and other parts of Europe and Asia. The largest is as big as a small rabbit, and the smallest fits into the palm of your hand. Only a few types of hamster can be kept as pets.

Hamsters are part of the mammal family, since they have warm blood and a hairy body.

Hamsters are mammals

All hamsters are part of the big group of animals called mammals. The mother hamster has babies that she feeds and looks after until they are able to take care of themselves. Hamsters are also members of the rodent family. Many hamsters come from areas where it is very hot during the day and then gets very cold at night. They are covered in hair, which helps to keep them warm.

The rodent family

Rats and mice, as well as guinea pigs and gerbils, are the hamster's closest relatives. These animals are all rodents. One thing that rodents have in common is their teeth. The teeth at the front of the mouth, called incisors, are very sharp and strong, which allows rodents to gnaw their food. Because a hamster's teeth are worn down by gnawing, they continue to grow throughout its life, unlike our teeth.

Hamster babies grow up fast. By the age of three months, they are fully grown.

Night animals

Hamsters sleep during the day, coming out of their burrows at night, when they are harder to see. In the wild, this helps to protect them from being caught for food by other animals. Since they are awake during the night, hamsters are often described as nocturnal animals. They have keen senses that help them to find their way in the dark.

Hamsters are nocturnal, and they are content to be left alone during the daytime.

A furry coat helps to keep the hamster warm.

Large ears allow hamsters to hear faint sounds clearly.

Hamsters have large eyes, but they cannot see very well in the daylight.

Strong back legs can support the hamster's weight when it sits up.

The hamster uses its front paws just like hands, to pick up and hold its food.

Whiskers are long, thick hairs that hamsters use to find their way around in the dark.

By sniffing around, hamsters can find food and discover if other hamsters have been in the area.

Hamster varieties

Most people are familiar with short-haired Syrian hamsters, which always used to be golden-colored, but these are not the only hamsters that make good pets. People have kept hamsters for many years, so all pet hamster varieties are friendly – unlike wild hamsters, which are shy around people. Pet hamsters can be several different colors now, so there are many to choose from. Hamsters can be long or short haired and some have shiny coats, too.

Short-haired Syrian hamsters

Most pet hamsters are short-haired Syrian hamsters, named after Syria, the country they come from. They have been bred in many colors, including white, cream, and gray.

This is the natural color of Syrian hamsters in the wilderness, and it is known as golden.

Long-haired Syrian hamsters

Hamsters with long coats are sometimes called Angoras, and they need much more grooming than hamsters with short coats. At first, when they are babies, Angoras have very short fur.

Syrian color varieties

Not all hamsters are one color. The popular tortoiseshell hamster has red and black fur. There are also chocolate and black hamsters, as well as banded hamsters, which are white mixed with another color.

Tortoiseshells have mixed coloring.

Long-haired hamsters have trailing fur, especially on the back of their bodies.

Dwarf Russian hamsters

These hamsters are smaller than Syrian hamsters and are more friendly toward each other. There are two types of dwarf Russian hamster. One is known as Campbell's and the other is the Winter White. They all have a dark line running down their backs.

Campbell's dwarf Russian hamsters are now being bred in different colors, the same as Syrians.

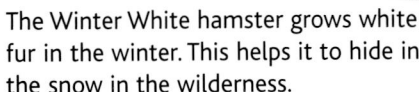

The Winter White hamster grows white fur in the winter. This helps it to hide in the snow in the wilderness.

Roborovski's hamsters

The smallest of the pet hamsters are called Roborovski's hamsters. They look a little bit like the dwarf Russian hamster, but have longer fur and are often not as friendly.

Chinese hamsters

Another type that are still rare is the Chinese hamsters, which have much longer tails than other hamsters. They also look a little bit like dwarf Russian hamsters, although the Chinese is bigger.

The smallest hamsters that are kept as pets are the Roborovski's hamsters. They originally came from the desert areas of China and Mongolia.

Small Chinese hamsters are becoming more popular as pets.

Choosing your hamster

It will be really exciting deciding which hamster to choose, but don't rush! You need to find a young hamster that is about four weeks old, because at this age, your new pet will be easier to tame. Hamsters are sold in many pet shops, but if you want a special color, you may have to go to a breeder. Ask an adult to search on the Internet for a hamster club in your area, so you can find a local breeder.

Syrian hamsters

It is very important that Syrian hamsters are kept on their own, because they will fight if put with another hamster. Remember that if you choose a Syrian hamster with markings on its coat, these will not change during your pet's life.

This Syrian hamster is much happier living alone. It should be alert and glowing with health. These are important factors to look for when choosing your pet.

Dwarf hamsters

You can keep two dwarf hamsters together, but buy them at the same time, so that they can settle down together. Then they will be less likely to fight. Two females or two males will get along well, but avoid choosing one of each, because they will have babies, which you might not be able to care for properly.

Two dwarf hamsters can live together happily.

Male or female?

It is very easy to tell whether an adult hamster is male or female, especially from a side view, without having to pick up your pet. Males have a steplike end to their bodies, and females have a much more rounded shape. Both make good pets.

You should ask the owner to pick up a young hamster to check if it is male or female. The gap between the openings on the underside of the body near the tail is bigger in males than females.

Adult male

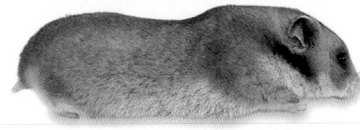

Adult female

Picking a healthy hamster

Young hamsters are often quite sleepy, especially during the day. But once they wake up, they should be very active and scamper around a lot. When examining a hamster, check that the eyes are bright and even in size, and that the nose is clean. The hamster should feel relatively plump all over, and the fur should not be dirty underneath the tail.

Young hamsters are often sleepy. Try to choose your hamster later in the day, when it will be more awake and lively.

Taking your hamster home

A special plastic carrying container with air vents is ideal for taking your hamster home. You can use this later when you need somewhere to keep your pet while you clean out its home. If you don't have one, however, you can bring your pet home in a cardboard box, but watch that it doesn't chew its way out on the way home.

Line the base of the carrier with some bedding, so that your new pet will be comfortable and can sleep on the way home.

When you get home, put the carrier on the floor of the cage and let your hamster come out on its own.

Your hamster's home

There are now many great ways for you to house your hamster. Some are tunnel systems that you can screw together. These are a little like the tunnels that wild hamsters inhabit. But you may prefer a cage, so you can catch and handle your new pet more easily.

Bedding and wood shavings will make your hamster's home cosy.

Choosing a cage

Your hamster will need plenty of space to climb around and keep active, so you should choose a large cage. There may be ladders for your hamster to scamper up, and platforms at different heights in taller cages. You will need to put wood shavings on the bottom of the cage for your hamster to burrow in.

Sleeping box

Give your hamster a box that it can use as a den to sleep in. Your hamster will curl up here and rest during the day. Use special, soft bedding that is safe for your pet. If the weather is hot, your hamster might move its bed out of the sleeping box for a while.

Cover the floor of the cage with untreated softwood shavings or crushed barley straw.

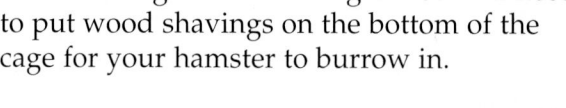

Exercise wheel

Hamsters are very active, so an important addition to your hamster's cage is a playwheel. This should be solid, rather than have open rungs, because one of your pet's feet might slip through a gap and become stuck. Be sure that it fits well, because wheels can be noisy. You may be kept awake by this at night if you keep your hamster's cage in your room.

Some wheels are freestanding, but others need to be secured to the side of the cage.

Where to keep your hamster

- Out of drafts

- Not in front of a window or in direct sunlight

- Away from radiators

- In a position where its home cannot be knocked over

- Out of reach of dogs and cats

Feeding equipment

Attach a drinking bottle to the side of the cage using the special clip. Position it just off the ground, where your hamster can reach it easily. Choose a sturdy food bowl that the hamster cannot knock over. Place this on the floor of the cage.

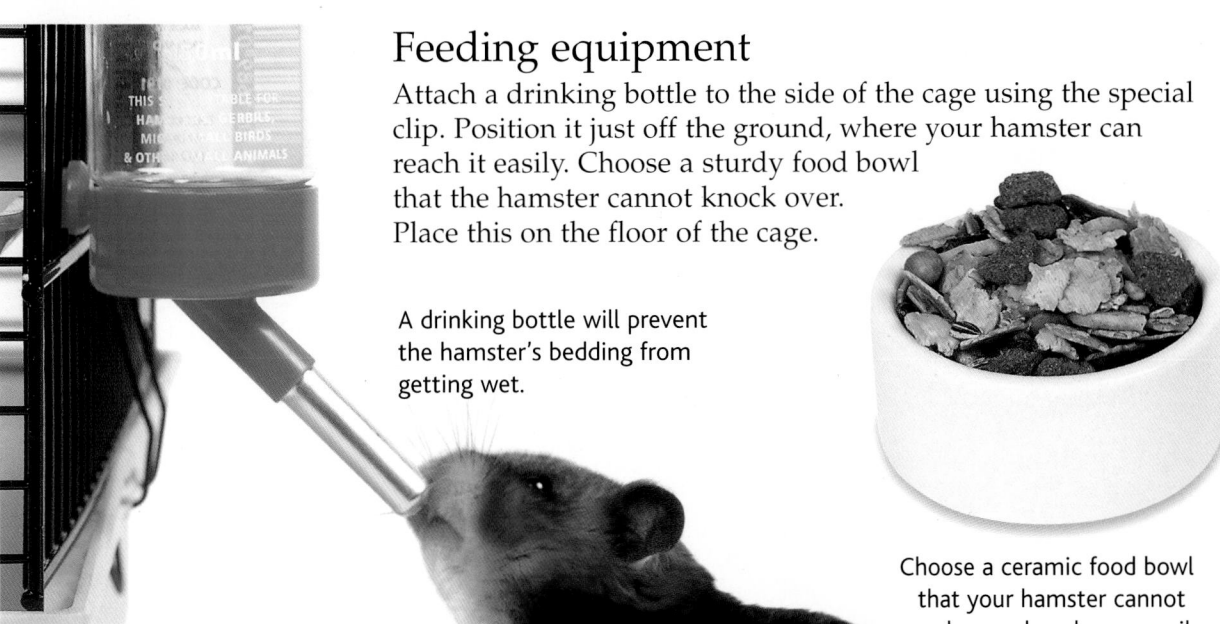

A drinking bottle will prevent the hamster's bedding from getting wet.

Choose a ceramic food bowl that your hamster cannot chew or knock over easily.

Feeding your hamster

Hamsters are very easy to feed, and you can buy special hamster food mixes at pet shops and some supermarkets. Hamsters eat a variety of different seeds and similar dried foods, but you should also offer your pet some fresh fruit or vegetables daily. Feed your hamster at the same time every day, for example, in the early evening. Also remember to change the water at the same time.

Hamsters like to eat a mixture of different seeds.

A hamster's face looks very swollen when it has a peanut in its pouch.

Collecting food

When a hamster eats, it usually stuffs lots of food into its mouth very quickly, instead of nibbling it. Hamsters feed in this way so that they are less likely to be caught by other animals in the wilderness. They are putting the food into big pouches inside their cheeks, instead of swallowing it. Then they carry their food back to their home in these pouches.

When a hamster empties its pouches, it may use its front paws to ease the food out. If you look in your hamster's house, you are likely to find stored food here, which it will eat when it is hungry.

Try to buy a hamster mix that has added vitamins and minerals.

Dried food

Most hamster food consists of a mixture of different seeds. These may include corn kernels and corn flakes, which are yellow in color, and peas flakes, which are light green. Look for sunflower seeds, too, which are usually striped, and peanuts, which might have papery, red skins but are white underneath.

Some mixes also have vitamins and minerals added to keep your hamster healthy. Hamsters usually eat about a tablespoon of dried food (7g) each day.

Fresh food

You can give your hamster all kinds of fresh food, from a sweet apple to a tangy tomato, as well as green vegetables such as cabbage. Only offer it one piece of fruit or vegetable a day, because it can cause a stomach upset if your hamster eats too much. Each morning, remove fresh food from the day before. Check your hamster's bed for leftovers stored there.

Chop up the fresh food for your hamster into chunks, but you don't need to bother peeling or coring it.

Special treats

Various treats are available for hamsters, and you can give these to your pet occasionally – but do not use them to replace its regular seed mix. Remember that some foods are not suitable for hamsters and can make them sick. Don't give your hamster candy of any kind, especially chocolate, or salty nuts or spicy food.

Some treats have hooks in them so you can hang them from the bars of the cage.

Handling

If you handle your hamster every day, it will quickly get used to being picked up. But don't try to pick it up right away. Allow your hamster to settle down in its new surroundings for a day or so before you start to handle it. Then, talk to your pet and let it smell your hand, so that it learns to trust you.

Don't get your hamster out of its cage until it is tame enough that you can handle it easily.

Feed your hamster some fresh food by hand, so that it gets used to seeing your hand.

Picking up your pet

Hamsters have sharp teeth and can give you a painful bite if you do not handle them properly. A hamster's eyesight is not as good as ours, and your pet can be frightened easily if you try to pick it up without warning. Once your hamster is tame, it is unlikely to bite you.

1 Let your hamster sniff your hand, so that it can smell your scent. It will soon learn that you will not hurt it.

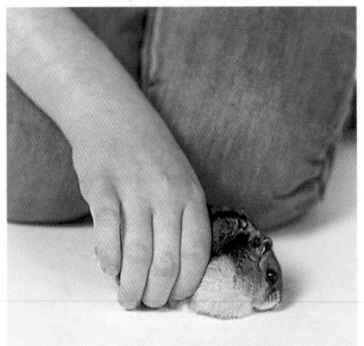

2 Gently scoop your hamster up from underneath with the fingers of one hand.

3 Cup your hamster in both hands, remembering not to hold it tightly. Stroking your hamster just in front of the ears may calm it down.

Playing with your hamster

If you want to bring your hamster out of its cage, be sure that if you have a cat or dog, it is out of the room and the door is shut. Otherwise it could attack your hamster.

It is safer to sit down on the floor or on a chair or sofa, so that if your hamster does escape, it will only fall a short distance onto a cushion and should not hurt itself.

Putting your pet back

Every time you put your hamster back in the cage, make sure that the door of the cage is securely shut afterward. It can be very hard to find a runaway hamster in the home, and your pet could easily end up being caught by the cat.

Let your hamster walk from hand to hand, keeping your hands close to your chest. Sitting on the floor is best, in case your hamster should fall.

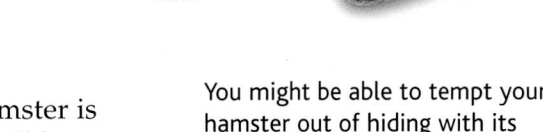

If your hamster escapes

The best time to search for a missing hamster is when it is getting dark, since your pet will be waking up and moving around then, so you might hear a noise.

You can set a special trap for your hamster if it is hungry. Place a ladder or a ramp leading up to a bucket lined with soft bedding, and put some food in the bottom. Hopefully, when your hamster tries to reach the food, it will fall into the bucket and will not be able to get out. If you're lucky, you will find your pet asleep here in the morning.

You might be able to tempt your hamster out of hiding with its favorite food.

15

Cleaning the cage

Every day you must remove any leftover fresh food that your pet has hidden in its house. You will need to clean your hamster's cage completely twice a week. If it is kept in a dirty home, your hamster is more likely to get sick and its cage will smell. Before you start cleaning the cage, catch your hamster and move it to its ventilated carrier. It will be safe here until you are ready to put it back in its clean quarters.

Wear rubber gloves whenever you clean out your hamster's cage to keep your hands clean.

Dismantling the cage

The base of most cages comes off easily from the wire part above. All you then need is a plastic bag, into which you can pour or scoop all the old cage floor covering and bedding.

Once the cage is clean, place a thick layer of shavings in the cage base.

Welcome home

Wipe the base with a piece of paper towel and then give your hamster a clean bed. Refill the food bowl and change the water, line the base with untreated wood shavings, and replace the top section of the cage. Now you can put your hamster back in the clean cage.

Disinfecting the cage

About once every two weeks, you should wash the cage, using a special disinfectant that is safe for hamsters. Empty the cage completely and then scrub the base and bars with a small brush.

Keep special scrub brushes and cloths that are just for cleaning your hamster's cage.

Rinsing the cage

After disinfecting the cage, you must rinse it very carefully and allow it to dry before putting it back together again. Wash plastic tubular cages in the same way.

Water bottle

You also need to clean out the water bottle every week with a bottle brush and wash the food bowl before refilling it.

The easiest way to clean the water bottle thoroughly is to use a bottle brush.

Remember to wash your hands!

It is important that, when you have cleaned out your hamster's home or just handled your pet, you wash your own hands thoroughly with soap right away. This should prevent any risk of you picking up an illness from your pet.

Away on vacation

Unfortunately, you will not be able to take your hamster on vacation with you unless you are staying at a friend's home just a short car trip away. But it is usually not difficult to find someone who can take care of your hamster. You could ask a friend to come to your house to feed your pet. Better yet, you might be able to take your hamster to your friend's house in its cage. Remember to clean the cage thoroughly before you go.

Ask a friend or an adult to help you carry your hamster's cage.

Always carry a hamster cage with your hands underneath it, so that it does not fall apart.

Don't forget to take your hamster's carrying container so that your friend has somewhere to put your hamster when cleaning the cage.

Write a list of instructions

It is easier if you have a friend who has kept a hamster of their own and knows what to do. Even so, write out a list of the food your hamster needs, how much to give and when to feed it.

In case of emergency

Do not forget to leave details of where you can be contacted in an emergency, as well as the phone number of your vet, in case your hamster gets sick.

Keeping your hamster healthy

Most hamsters stay healthy throughout their lives if they are kept clean and well-fed. But if you think that your pet could be sick, then it is very important to contact a vet for advice as soon as possible. Hopefully, your hamster can then be treated and will get better quickly. Most hamsters live for about two or three years. As your hamster grows older, its coat will most likely get thinner. This is normal.

Checking claws

Hamster claws seldom become too long, since they are worn down as the hamster climbs around its home, but you should check them regularly and get them trimmed if necessary.

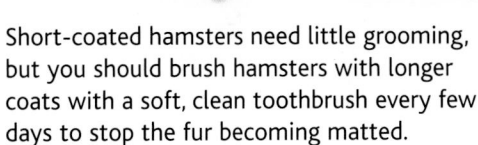

Short-coated hamsters need little grooming, but you should brush hamsters with longer coats with a soft, clean toothbrush every few days to stop the fur becoming matted.

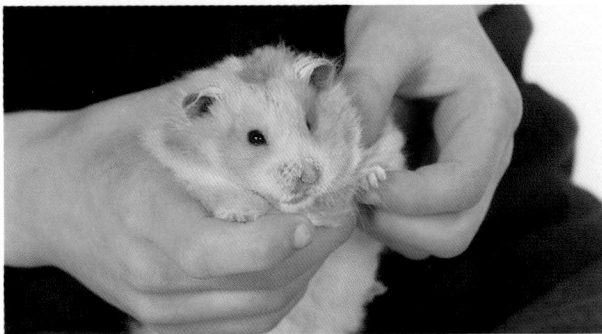

Taking Care of teeth

A hamster's teeth can grow too long if it cannot gnaw on hard surfaces and wear them down. This is why you should always put a chew, made of special colored wood, or a gnawing log in your hamster's cage, and possibly a mineral block, too.

  If your hamster is having difficulty eating. It may be that its teeth need to be trimmed, and the vet can do this for you.

Hamsters need to gnaw on things such as this untreated apple tree branch, to prevent their teeth from growing too long.

This edition is published by Lorenz Books

Lorenz Books is an imprint of Anness Publishing Ltd
Hermes House, 88–89 Blackfriars Road, London SE1 8HA
tel. 020 7401 2077; fax 020 7633 9499
www.lorenzbooks.com
info@anness.com

© Anness Publishing Ltd 2002

Published in the USA by Lorenz Books, Anness Publishing Inc.
27 West 20th Street, New York, NY 10011; fax 212 807 6813

Published in Australia by Lorenz Books, Anness Publishing Pty Ltd
Level 1, Rugby House, 12 Mount Street, North Sydney, NSW 2060
tel. (02) 8920 8622; fax (02) 8920 8633

This edition distributed in the UK by Aurum Press Ltd
tel. 020 7637 3225; fax 020 7580 2469

This edition distributed in the USA by National Book Network
tel. 301 459 3366; fax 301 459 1705; www.nbnbooks.com

This edition distributed in Canada by General Publishing
tel. 416 445 3333; fax 416 445 5991; www.genpub.com

This edition distributed in New Zealand by David Bateman Ltd
tel. (09) 415 7664; fax (09) 415 8892

A CIP catalogue record for this book is available from the British Library.

Publisher: Joanna Lorenz
Managing Editor: Linda Fraser
Editor: Sarah Uttridge
Designer: Linda Penny
Photographer: Bruce Tanner

The publishers would like to thank Grace Crissell, Eilish Main and Ben McLoughlin for modeling for this
book. With special thanks to David Baglin of the British Hamster Association for providing the hamsters.
Picture credit: NHPA /Daniel Heuclin 7br
1 3 5 7 9 10 8 6 4 2